THIS BOOK BELONGS TO:

....

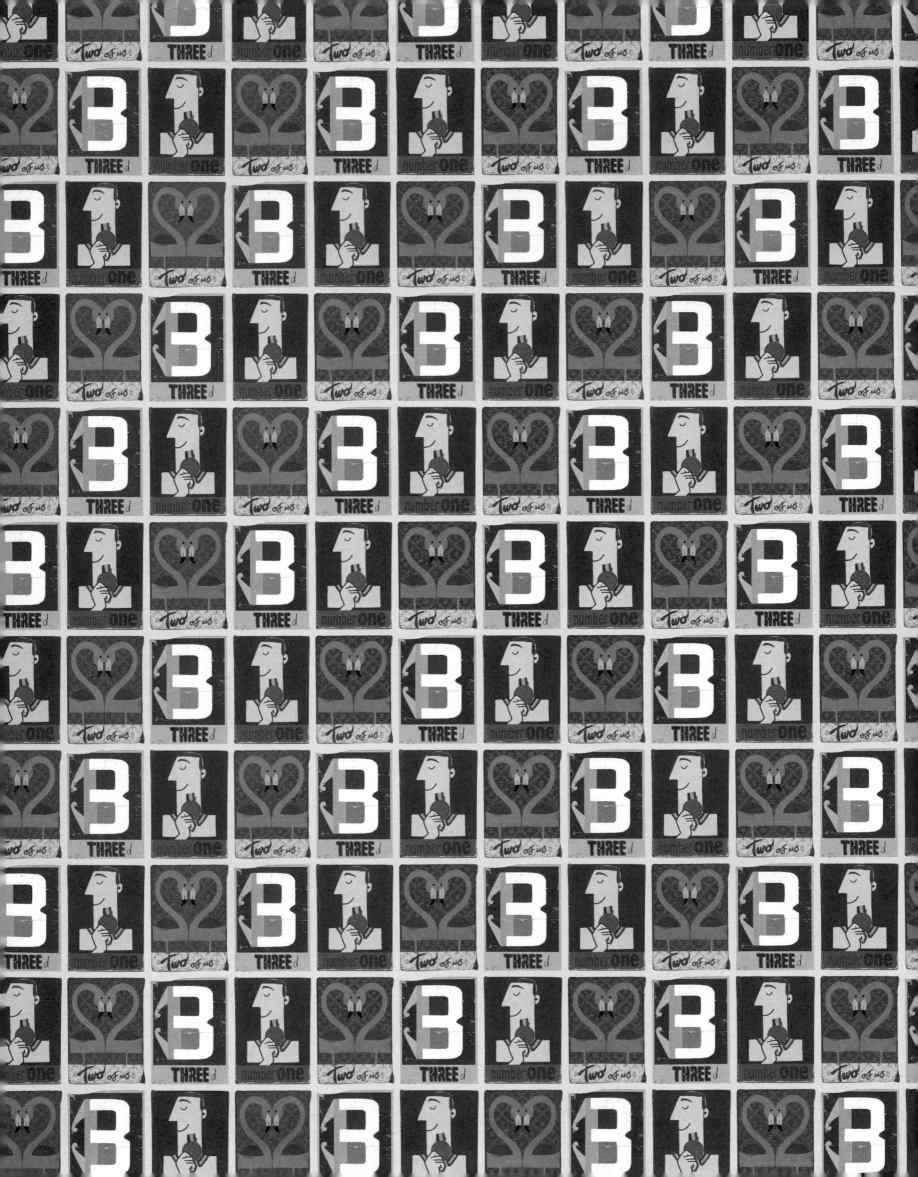

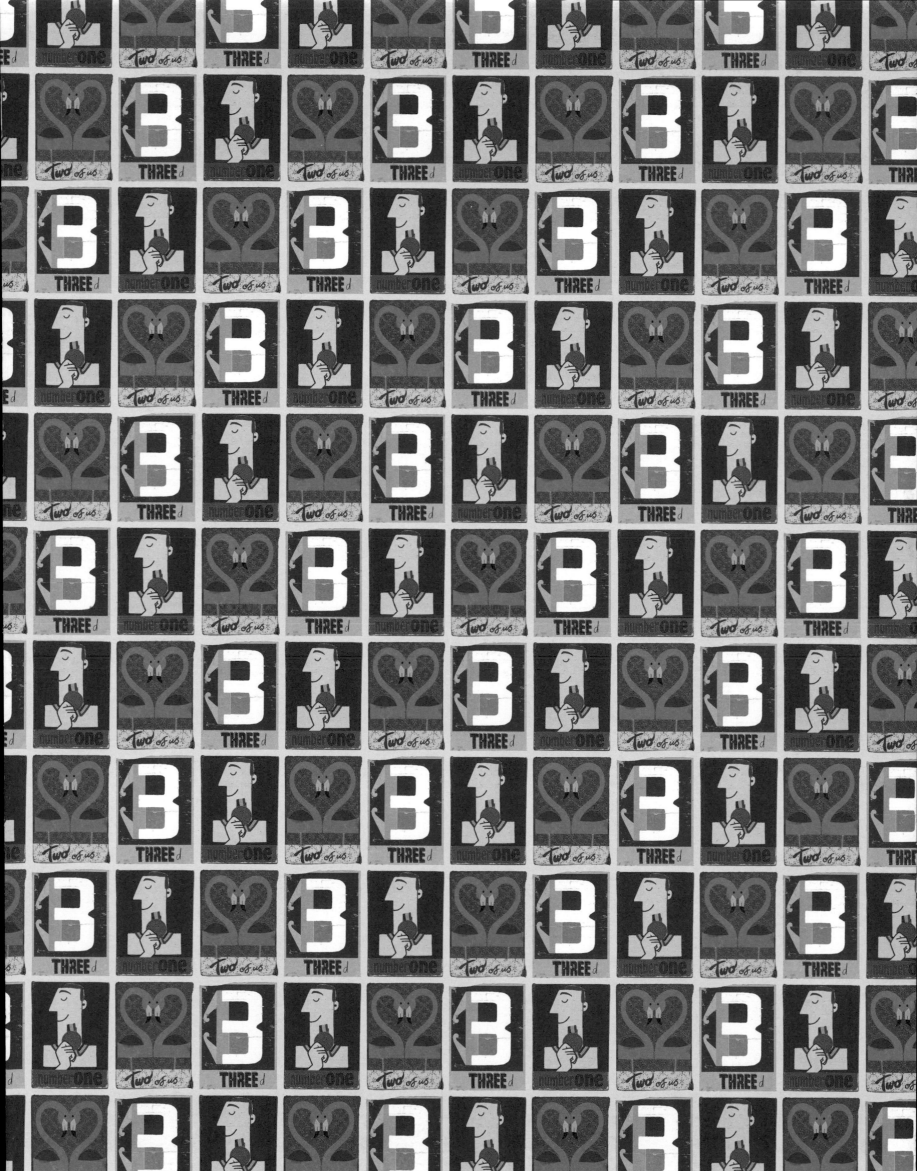

I started working on Numbers the year after I had finished Alphabet. It immediately became apparent that attaching meaning to numbers would prove more of a challenge than the alphabet. Not to mention the fact that maths was one of my least favourite subjects at school. I hope I have succeeded, where my teacher Mr Housden failed, in making numbers fun. In the end, I really enjoyed working on this book.

Originally from Nottingham, now based in London, I have been working as a full-time illustrator since 2006: I hold my pen in an unusual manner and was never 'corrected' by any teachers at school.

I work on commissions in advertising, publishing, editorial and design for clients including The Southbank Centre, The Guardian, The French Tourist Board, It's Nice That, Nineteen Seventy Three Ltd, Templar Publishing, Vanity Fair, The New Yorker and Warner/Chappell.

My inspiration comes from mid-century design and illustration. My work has been described as being retro-modern. I use old books, postcards and pieces of paper for the backgrounds. Often, for example, I will buy an old book from a charity shop just to use its back page.

For my sister, Tina; and nieces Natalie, Eryn and Francesca.

Paul thurlby

An imprint of Hachette Children's Group

NUMBERS

Hodder
Children's
Books

An imprint of Hachette Children's Group

ZERO

1

ONE

2
TWO

3
THREE

THREE d

4
FOUR

The **Fab FOUR**

HIGH FIVE

6

SIX

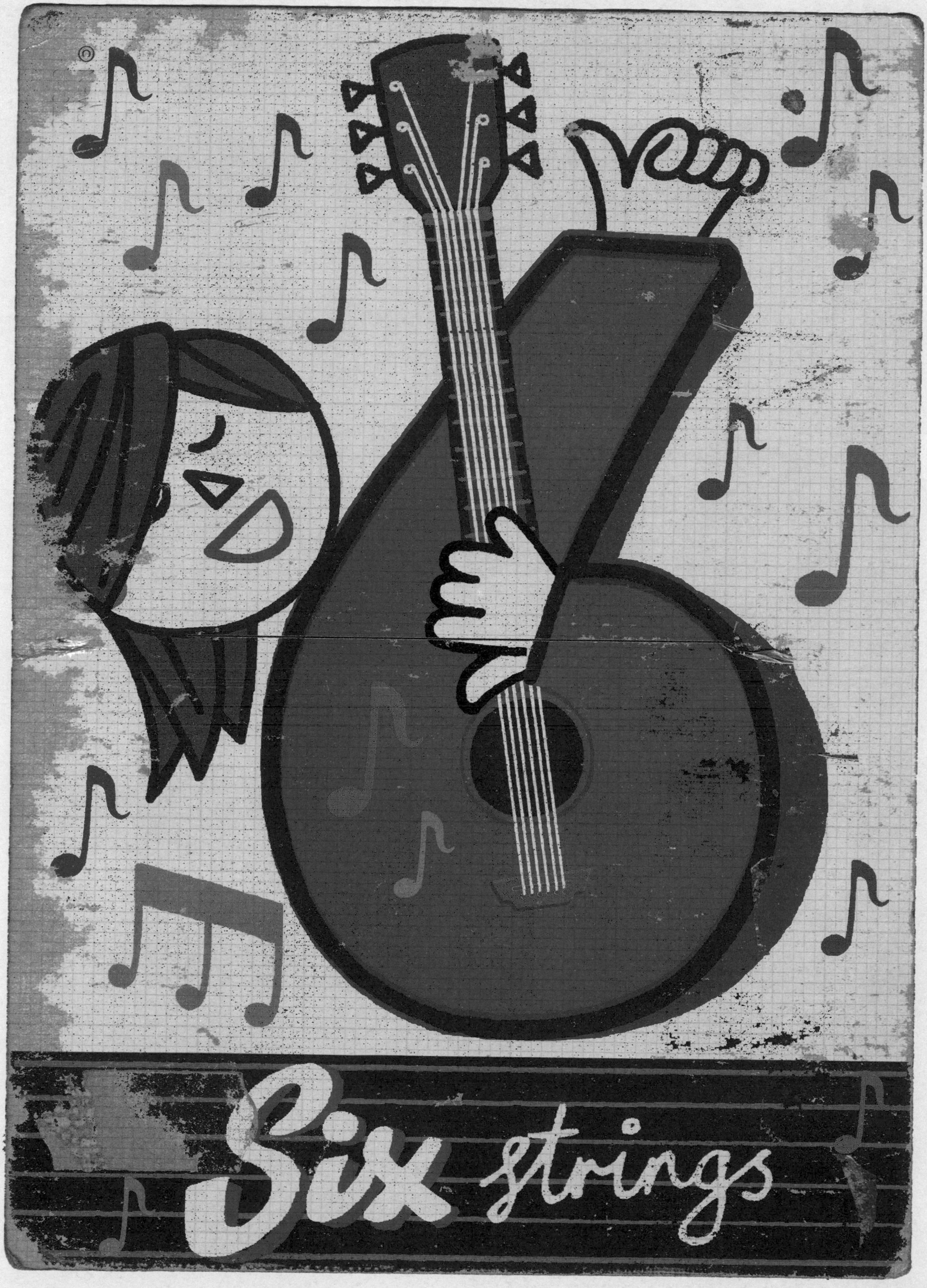
Six strings

7
SEVEN

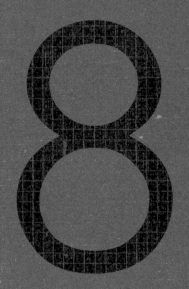

EIGHT

9

NINE

10
TEN

Perfect **TEN**

20
TWENTY

TWENTY

MILES PER HOUR

30
THIRTY

40
FORTY

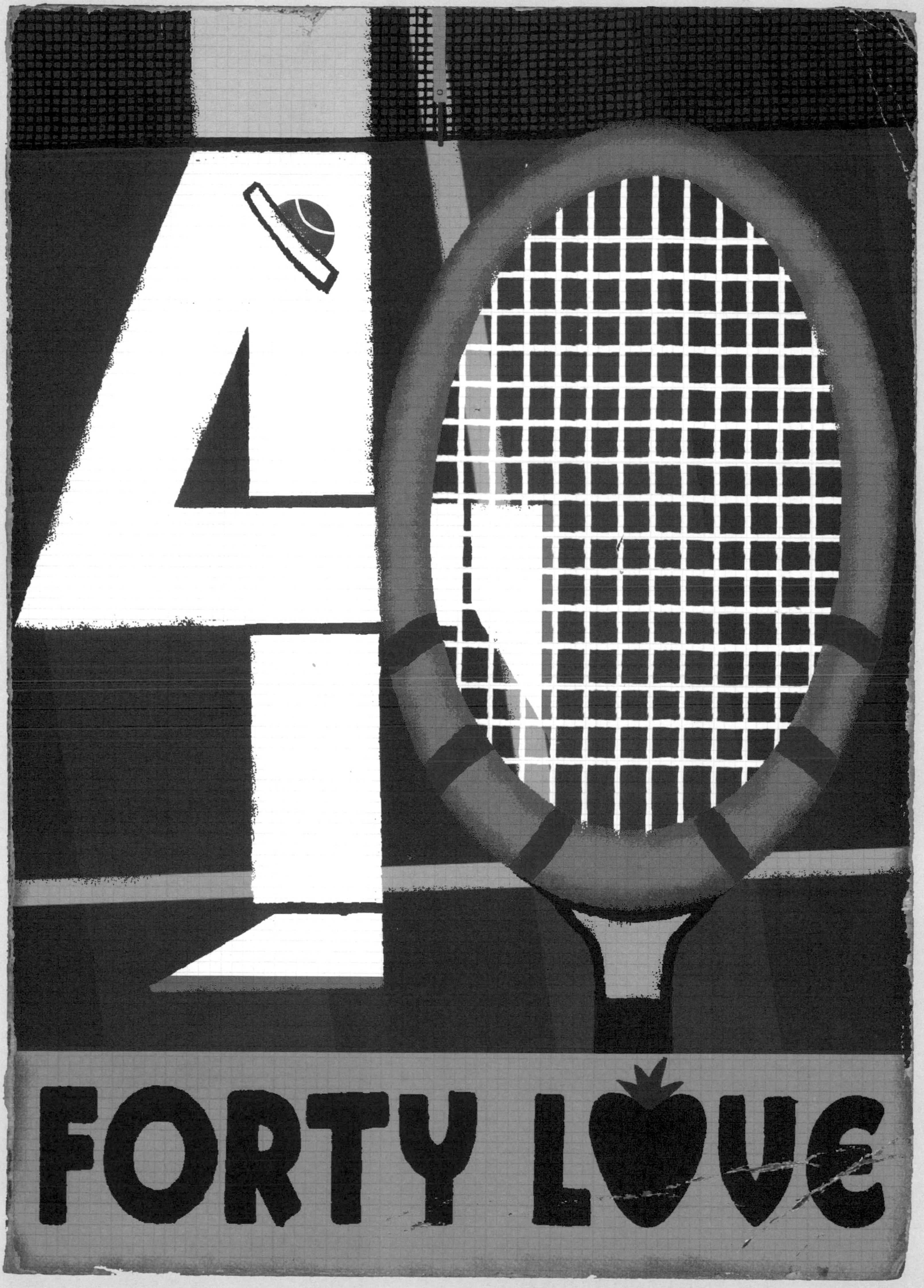
FORTY LOVE

50
FIFTY

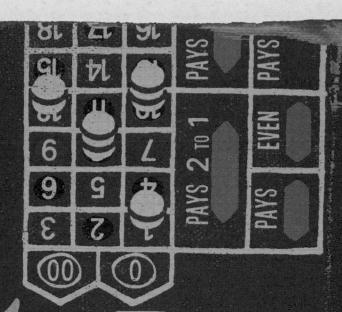

60
SIXTY

SIXTY SECONDS

70
SEVENTY

DISCO SEVENTY

80
EIGHTY

AROUND THE WORLD IN

EIGHTY

DAYS

90
NINETY

NINETY DEGREES

100
ONE
HUNDRED

ONE HUNDRED
PER CENT

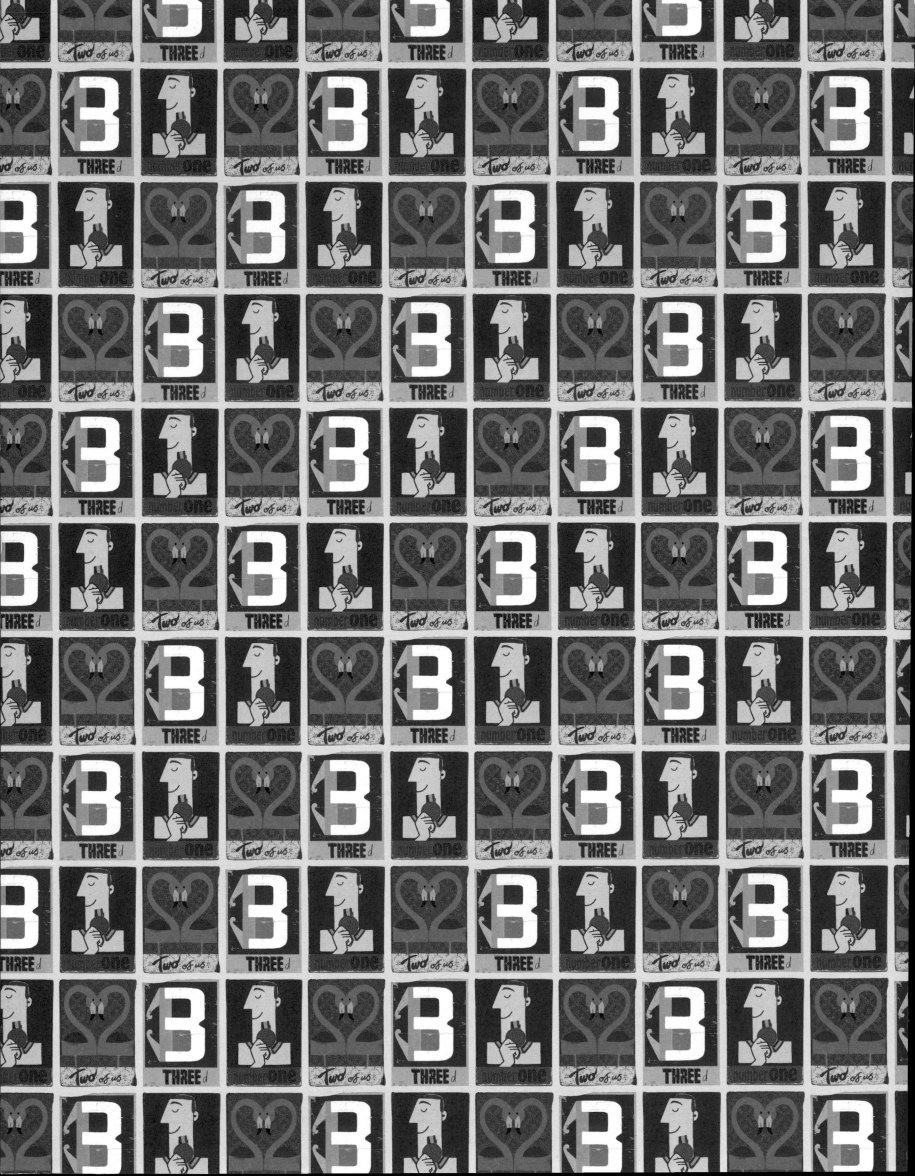

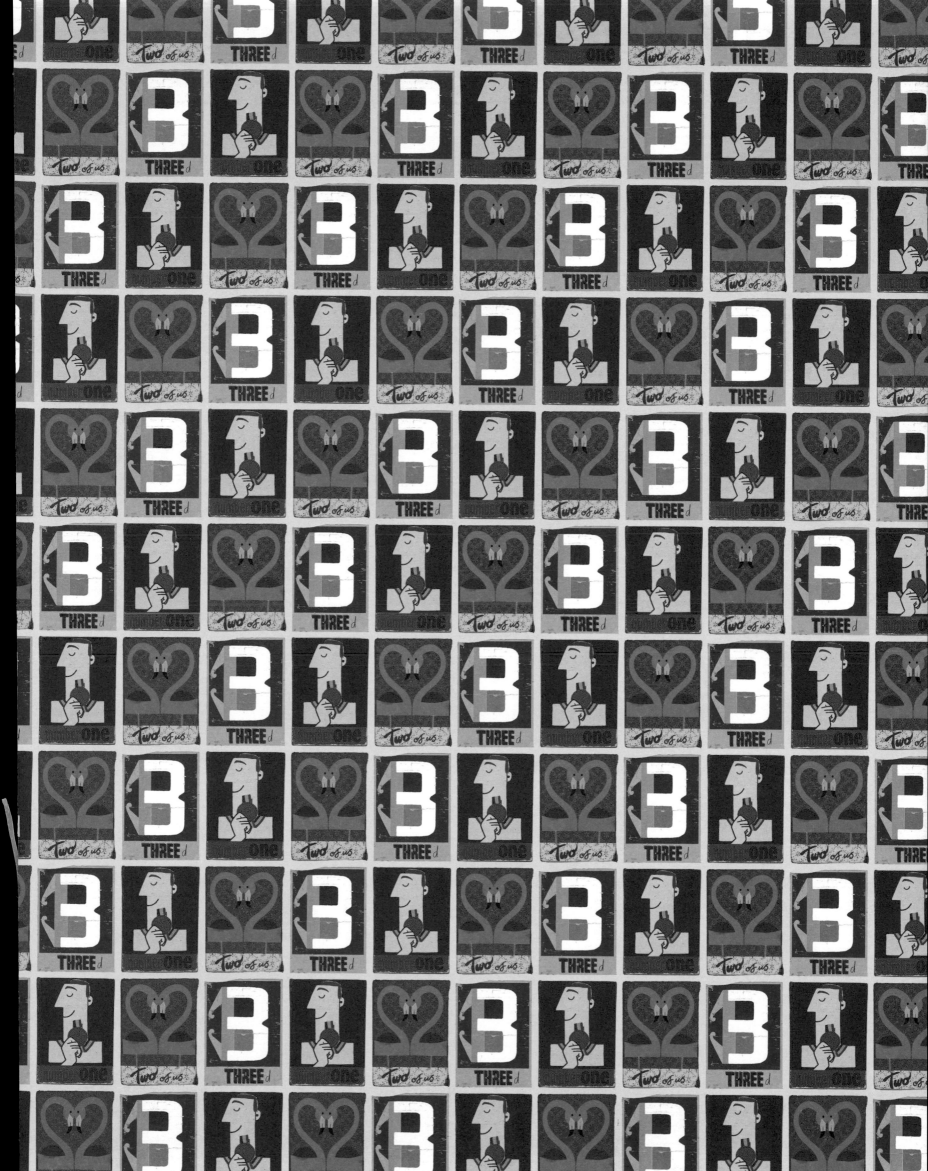

WWW.PAULTHURLBY.COM

FIRST PUBLISHED IN 2014 BY HODDER CHILDREN'S BOOKS
THIS PAPERBACK EDITION FIRST PUBLISHED IN 2015
COPYRIGHT © PAUL THURLBY 2014

A CATALOGUE RECORD OF THIS BOOK IS AVAILABLE FROM THE BRITISH LIBRARY.

ISBN: 978 1 444 91876 2

PRINTED IN CHINA

HODDER CHILDREN'S BOOKS, AN IMPRINT OF HACHETTE CHILDREN'S GROUP
PART OF HODDER & STOUGHTON
CARMELITE HOUSE, 50 VICTORIA EMBANKMENT, LONDON EC4Y 0DZ
AN HACHETTE UK COMPANY. WWW.HACHETTE.CO.UK